For The Children's Sake:

For The Children's Sake:

Parenting Together after the Marriage Ends

A little book of *wise words* for divorced parents

Brenda Dozier, Ph.D., LMFT, LPC

iUniverse, Inc.
New York Lincoln Shanghai

For The Children's Sake:
Parenting Together after the Marriage Ends

iUniverse, Inc.

For information address:
iUniverse, Inc.
2021 Pine Lake Road, Suite 100
Lincoln, NE 68512
www.iuniverse.com

Information in this book is not intended to replace the services of an attorney, mediator, or qualified mental health professional.

Names and identifying characteristics of individuals in this book have been changed to protect confidentiality.

ISBN: 0-595-31726-X

Printed in the United States of America

This book is dedicated to my lovely daughter, Lori Renee Hinkle, who has been a constant reminder that there are rewards when parents *act right* after divorce. Without a doubt, the most joyful day in my life was the day Lori was born. She had to make many sacrifices while I was in graduate school and she was always forgiving of my shortcomings and proud of my accomplishments. It has been so delightful to see her grow into the fine woman she is today, and I look forward to watching her as she continues to savor the gifts of life. Thank you, Lori. *I love you. God Loves You.*

Contents

Acknowledgment

I must acknowledge all the families who have offered themselves as gifts to me. They opened up very sacred places in their hearts and souls and so willingly shared their hopes, fears, and dreams. Adults and children in my office taught me the struggles of building two homes after divorce strikes, when many times it would have been easier for them to have thrown in the towel. The years and tears I spent with these families made it possible for me to write this book.

Introduction

For the Children's Sake: Parenting Together after the Marriage Ends was written for you. You long to decrease the pain your separation or divorce is causing your children. But you also know that sometimes it is difficult to soothe your children when you are still recovering from the aftermath of divorce. Keep in mind that the first year is the most difficult for you and your children. You will find yourself doing, thinking, and saying things that you never thought you would do, think, or say. Be forgiving of yourself; apologize to your children when it is warranted, and most importantly, keep yourself focused on the ultimate goals of investing in your relationship with your child, enhancing your child's well-being, and building your own self-worth.

For many years, children of all ages and divorcing adults have shared their experiences with me in my therapy office. Some have taught me how to help parents preserve parent-child relationships after divorce strikes. Others have shown me how parent-child relationships can be destroyed by angry, vindictive parents. I have put together this little book as a collection of some of these *wise words* that will help you help your children during this traumatic time.

For the Children's Sake is not a replacement for legal representation, divorce mediation, or counseling. Instead, it will answer some questions many divorcing or separating parents have about how to help their children survive divorce.

Effects of Divorce on Children

Divorce hurts children. The degree of the pain, however, is directly associated with the continued conflict between the parents. This is not to say that children from divorced homes with parents who argue frequently are the only ones who suffer. Severe parental conflict also harms children who reside in homes with both parents.

There are many significant life events that challenge the human being's well-being. Divorce is ranked number two. Only the death of a loved one is rated as more traumatizing. How children react and adjust after their parents separate and/or divorce is related in part to how the adults interact with one another around parenting issues. It is also associated with the quality of the parent-child relationship. In addition, adjustment depends on the developmental stage and chronological age of the child. Sometimes parents, teachers, and other caregivers notice that following divorce, a child acts out, withdraws, or regresses to an earlier stage/age. Many times parents blame one another for their child's problems. It may have nothing to do with what is occurring in either home. Instead, it may be responses typical of a certain developmental stage. The information below will assist you in understanding what your child is going through.

Infants and Toddlers (Birth to Three Years):

The primary tasks for infants and toddlers are to trust their caregivers and to develop secure, attached relationships with them. Young babies require a lot of attention from mothers and fathers. Consistency in caring for babies is critical. Ideally, the infant needs both parents to feed, bathe, and spend time holding and talking with them on a daily basis.

Divorce challenges for the infant or toddler: Feeling of loss of parent and familiar environment. The child may cling to both parents during this stage. Many times they will act out the anger or hurt they may feel about the change in their family because they don't know how to verbalize emotions.

How you can help infants and toddlers: These negative feelings of loss are diminished when parents can alternate every other day or share time in a single day to care for the little one. Here are some do's and don'ts that will help you help your infant or toddler:

Do's:

- Be civil to the other parent in front of the infant/toddler.

- Develop schedules in caring for the baby, which allow both parents frequent and regular intervals.

- Gradually move the baby from the familiar home to the second home for overnights.

- Send a toy or other attachment object from your home with the baby to the other parent's home.

Don'ts:

- Fight with the other parent in front of the baby.

- Have long periods of time in parenting schedules that result in the infant/toddler being primarily with only one of you for days at a time.

Preschoolers (Three years to Six Years):

Children in the preschool stage are faced with the developmental task of learning how to do things for themselves and developing their self-identity. Preschool age children are often magical in their way of thinking, they love to explore the environment, and they use fantasy play. Children who have successfully moved through infancy and toddler hood are secure and they trust their parents will meet their physical and safety needs.

Divorce challenges: Secure feelings often are replaced with insecure ones after separation. Clinging to a parent or acting like an infant is not an unusual response to parental divorce for this age group. Magical thinking may include believing the divorce was their fault. For example, a three-year-old states, "*I was bad and Daddy left.*" Because preschool aged children are egocentric, they sometimes do think they are responsible for the actions of others. Likewise, they may try all sorts of responses, such as negative behaviors, to get the two parents back together.

How you can help your preschooler:

- Tell your child the divorce was not her/his fault.

- Maintain parenting schedules that allow the child to be with each of you every few days. Know that your young child may fear losing both of you.

- Allow your child to embellish stories as his/her way of expression. Don't take all ideas literally; it may be the preschooler's way of releasing frustration.

- Place a picture of the other parent in the child's bedroom in your home.

- In both homes, decorate a shoe box with your preschooler and put the other parent's name or picture on it. When the child misses the absent parent, he/she can draw a picture, write a letter, etc. Place the mail in the child's bag when making the exchange to the other home.

The School-Age Child (Six Years to 13 Years):

Developing competency, morals, and peer acceptance are critical issues faced by the school-age child. This is a rapid time of growth: physically, mentally, emotionally, morally, and socially.

Divorce challenges: The school-age child often feels loyalty conflicts when their parents divorce. They sometimes go through stages of siding with one parent and then the other. Some of these children are ashamed and embarrassed about the divorce and may even try to reconcile their parents. Many children feel deep grief and they may be overly concerned about how their world is going to change. They may worry about finances, which parent is going to take care of them, and they may even fear a parent will remarry.

How to help your school-age child: Your child at this age needs both parents to be dependable and to serve as role models while they face multiple developmental tasks. Parents must understand that the child's forming an alliance with one parent and later on the other, is a typical reaction. Make sure you do not use this response as ammunition in a custody battle and ask your child to choose who he/she wants to live with. Here are some basic do's and don'ts:

Do's:

- Let your child know he/she does not have to choose one parent over the other one. Assure her/him that both of you will continue an active role.

- Listen to your child's needs, concerns, and fears. It is important for you to create an atmosphere that is safe for your child to express frustrations about living between two homes.

- Support your school-age child's relationship with the other parent.

- Allow your child to be a child.

- Attend as many extracurricular activities your child participates in as you can. Assure your child that both parents can be there without any concern of either parent creating a *public scene* or embarrassment to him/her.

- Know your school-age child's friends and their parents. To do this, you must stay involved with your child on a frequent basis.

- Maintain a civil and courteous relationship with the other parent in front of your child.

- Stay in touch with teachers and ask them to let you know if your child's behaviors or academic performance changes.

- Maintain as much consistency in lifestyle as possible (i.e., same school, neighborhood).

- Be flexible with parenting schedules to help meet the child's social growth.

- Continue with the mailbox idea. Use it to put copies of report cards, activity schedules, etc. that you receive when your child is with you. This will insure that your child gets the need met of having both of you involved in all aspects of his/her life.

- Use a careful plan to integrate new significant adults into your child's world.

Don'ts:

- Bash the other parent in front of your child.

- Judge your child's feelings, concerns or complaints about the divorce.

- Avoid or withdraw from your child.

- Allow your child to withdraw from you.

- Expect your child to be the adult and contact you if he/she wants to spend time with you.

- Put your child in the middle of your divorce war. It is not a child's place to ask the other parent for money, favors, etc.

- Withhold information about your child's school events and activities from the other parent. If you do, you are hurting your child, not just your former spouse.

Adolescents (13 Years to 18 Years):

During this life phase, teenagers are searching for their own individuality by moving away from the family and forming closer relations with their peers.

Divorce challenges: Often, teens worry about one parent and take on the role of the absent parent. Some even form sides with one parent against the other. The divorce may make the adolescent question their own intimate relationships and feel unsure about having a stable and satisfying marriage themselves.

How to help adolescents cope with parental divorce: Stay involved in your teenager's life. Know friends, attend events and activities, and spend private time with him/her. Basic do's and don'ts include:

Do's:

- Keep the communication line open with your adolescent.

- Coordinate with the other parent to prevent your teen from practicing manipulative behaviors.

- Take care of your divorce recovery needs with other adults or a caring professional rather than relying on your teen as your counselor or confidante.

- Find a mental health professional, youth minister, or other trusting adult for your teen to talk to if she/he doesn't want to talk to you about the divorce.

- Be flexible with your parenting arrangement to adapt to your teen's developmental needs.

- Allow your adolescent to give input into parenting schedules.

Don'ts:

- Expect your adolescent to initiate all conversations with you.

- Condemn, ignore, or attack your teen's thoughts and feelings about the divorce.

- Think that your teen is *old enough* to deal with divorce issues without experiencing any problems.

- Involve your adolescent in your divorce battle.

- Rely on your teen for your emotional support.

- Use bribery as a means to get your adolescent to choose your side against the other parent.

- Let your teen make all the decisions about spending time with you.

College Age/Young Adulthood:

This is a challenging and exciting time as young people work on becoming more autonomous. They struggle with developing intimate relationships, establishing career goals, and comparing a variety of worldviews to their family-of-origin backgrounds.

Divorce challenges: Your college student/young adult may become frustrated with splitting holiday and vacation times. Many of them get tired of trying to please so many adults (e.g., both parents, new stepparents, extended family members). They may begin to feel anxious about their own future relationships and marriage.

How you can help:

- Give your college age/young adult assurance that both parents will participate in their significant life events such as graduations, celebrations, and weddings.

- Allow your child to have an active voice in holiday and vacation plans.

- Encourage continued interactions between your child and both parents.

- Tell your college age/young adult that both of you know divorce is hard on her/him. Encourage your child to seek professional help if it is needed.

Now that you have identified your child s developmental challenges to divorce and learned how you can help reduce the pain divorce recovery brings, it will benefit you to take a look at what children, teens, and college-age young adults have said about the aftermath of parental divorce.

Words of Wisdom from Children

Below are some direct expressions children of various ages have made in my therapy office. The spelling represents the children's authentic written or verbal statements. These quotes lend support to why divorcing adults must separate their feelings about one another from their roles as parents.

"I just want mommy and daddy to be friends."

Benjamin, age 7 (parents divorced for three years)

"Dear daddy, I want you to quilt drinking, quilt saying bad things to mommy when I'm in front of you, go do your best!"

Jennifer, age 10 (parents divorced for six months)

"My mamma says my daddy is real mean and I shouldn't be nice to him."

Timothy, age 8 (divorce in-process)

"Daddy told me that me and him are going to California and I won't ever have to see my mamma because she ain't good for me."

Justin, age 6 (divorce in-process)

"My mom is so sad and I am the only person she talks to. See, I am tougher than she is so I have to be strong to help her."

Melissa, age 13 (parents divorced for 10 months)

"I hate it when he questions me about Mom's social life. He knows she is dating John. But he can't stand it that she is happy. He expects me to tell him every time Mom and John have a date. I don't want to talk to him or have dinner with him anymore."

Lauren, age 16 (parents divorced for four years)

"I don't want daddy to go."

Matthew, age 5 (divorce in-process)

"I just don't want to be with him right now. My mom needs me. I finally had enough of his criticism. My mom has a lawyer who is going to get it changed so I can live with her. He thinks this is her idea but it is mine. I want to be with my mom all the time."

Lawrence, age 15 (parents divorced for 10 years)

"I feel like a rubber band...Mamma pulls me to her and Daddy pulls me to him."

Erica, age 12 (parents divorced for two years)

"My own book about DEVORCE:

It's hard being the only child especially if your parents are DEVORCED! The older you get, you'll get used to it as you get older. It kind of gets on my nervers driving back and forth, back and forth to my Dad's house and my Mom's house and it is not fare having your parents DEVORCED! If I had to chose to live with my mom or dad, I would go live with my grandma and granddaddy and never go back! I hate my parents being DEVORCED!"

Caroline, age 9 (parents divorced three years)

"My Rules:

1. Don't put me in the middle.

2. Quit arguing.

3. Quit saying bad things.

4. Talk polite to each other/about each other.

5. All parents (step and real) come to my activities.

6. Braeck bad habits like smoking and drinking."

Caroline, age 9 (same as above)

"I called my Dad and asked him to come to my graduation party. He said he would love to as long as my Mom didn't bring that s.o.b. she is married to. I called my Mom and invited her and she said she couldn't come if my Dad brought that whore he is living with. I told both of them that my fiancé's parents were going to be my new parents and neither of them was going to come to my graduation or my wedding! I finally had enough! They have been divorced for ten years and they still hate each other."

Alan, age 26

"When my first baby was born my mother refused to come to the hospital because my father was going to be there. I thought I would get used to it but it has been 18 years and now that I have children it spills over onto them. My parents live close by one another and since I live away it would be nice if they would take the kids to each other's home in the summer but they won't. I have to coordinate all of that. My kids have started to pick up on how weird things are."

Julie, age 34

"The thing I am most sick of is trying to please everybody. I have to please daddy and my stepmom when I am there, mamma and my stepdad when I stay with them. And then there are my grandparents. Sometimes I just don't want to go home for vacations or holidays."

Jimmy, age 20 (parents divorced for four years)

"Daddy and my stepmom had a new baby and it is a girl. I don't want to go to his house anymore. I'm scared I am not his little princess anymore."

Laura, age 16 (parents divorced for two years)

Summary of Parenting Together

The previous sections outlined the uniqueness of particular child life cycle stages, how divorce affects children during those phases, and some direct expressions made by children of divorced parents. Below is a summary of do's and don'ts for parents to remember regardless of child age or of time since divorce.

Parenting Together After Divorce: Must Do's

- Spend regular, consistent time with your children.

- Know your child's developmental age/stage issues, challenges, and needs.

- Maintain familiar routines as much as possible (limit the losses).

- Be flexible and adaptable.

- Maintain children's interactions with your extended family.

- Have a careful plan to integrate new significant others to children.

- Attend children's activities (i.e., sports, arts, church) and visit schools.

- Keep commitments and promises made to children.

- Speak directly to the other parent rather than having the child as the go-between.

- Pay attention to tone when talking to the other parent in front of the children.

- Allow the other parent to parent his/her own way when abuse or neglect is absent.

- Make sure the children know the divorce was not their fault.

- Get adult support rather than relying on children for emotional help.

- Receive help from a family systems Two-Home Family divorce expert.

Parenting Together After Divorce: Must Don'ts:

- Don't ignore or avoid children when upset with the other parent.

- Don't manipulate, pressure, or lie in order to make children take sides.

- Don't ask children who they want to live with.

- Don't expose children to your arguments, abusive behavior, or conflicts.

- Don't rely on children for emotional support.

- Don't ask children to read legal documents about the divorce.

- Don't bash the other parent in front of the children.

- Don't force new significant others onto children.

- Don't bash other parent's extended family members.

- Don't be rigid.

How Can We Parent Together?
We Can't Stand One Another!

One-third to one-half of former spouses maintain intense anger toward one another a decade after the divorce is final. Even so, adults may replace spouses at anytime, but children cannot replace original (i.e., birth or adoptive) parents. You can parent together even if you don't like your ex as a human being and it is difficult to be in the same room with her/him. First, you have to address the roadblocks that are in your way. These roadblocks are outlined below.

After you identify your roadblocks and work through them, then you can begin to build a *business partnership* with your ex. This new partnership is governed by both of you and is restricted to the business of parenting and it will allow you to do what is best for your children. All children deserve to have two parents at all times. If they cannot have both parents in the same home, then having them in separate homes is critical. As a family therapist and a divorce specialist, that is what my Two-Home Family model is about. So, you don't have to like your ex, nor do you have to spend a lot of time with him/her. But, you do have to have a plan for parenting. Maintaining a home and family is like running a business, so you must have a business plan that gives job descriptions for parents and policies and procedures that outline how the two of you are going to raise your children.

Roadblock: Attachment Between Ex-Spouses

Where do you begin in identifying your roadblocks? Determine first how you may still be *attached* to your former spouse. Perhaps you didn't want the divorce. Or maybe you did initiate leaving but feel guilty and ashamed. It takes time to heal from the hurt divorce causes. Attachment is normal in close relationships and over time can result in continued positive or negative feelings toward the attachment figure.

Letting go of this attachment is much easier said than done, and it may continue long after the judge has signed your divorce decree. The important thing is to realize that your pain may be preventing you from attending to your child's needs. Here are some ways to end your marriage so that you can begin to co-parent with your ex-spouse and tend to your child's needs:

- Get professional help from a therapist who is qualified to address the myriad of ways divorce affects individuals and families.

- Find a support group where other adults are experiencing separation or divorce (many churches offer singles ministries; mental health professionals offer divorce recovery groups for children and adults).

- Stop telling friends and family members how evil your ex is. Negative talk breeds negative feelings.

- Set new life goals. View this challenge as an opportunity to grow and become more of what you would like to become. You may embark on a new career or find new hobbies.

- See your medical doctor if you are having serious physical symptoms of depression or anxiety. A mental health professional can assist you.

- Allow yourself time and space to grieve. Grief is unique. Your way may not be the same as other people you know.

- Give up bad habits that are keeping you down. Replace them with constructive habits.

- Make yourself smile at everyone you see. Everyday. Pretend that you are on top of the world! Before long you will be!

Roadblock: Economics

Other roadblocks may prevent you from developing a co-parenting arrangement with your former spouse. For example, *economics* may have to be worked through. A mediator can help you resolve issues around property, assets, and money.

Roadblock: Parenting Styles

- Your attitude about the differences in parenting styles may keep you from co-parenting. Sometimes it may be that you don't think your ex acts right because he/she doesn't parent like you do. We all grew up with adults who had certain styles in their parenting behaviors. If the two of you are similar in your parenting beliefs about certain things like bedtimes, curfews, household chores, academic performance, etc., your children will be less likely to manipulate either of you. However, as long as abuse or neglect isn't taking place, it is not harmful to your children if the two of you run your homes differently. In other words, you and your children will be happier if you allow your ex to *parent* her/his own way. Below are three basic parenting styles. See which one fits you. What about your ex?

- *Hippie Parents*

Hippie homes have a major rule: There are no rules. Children and adults cross over each other's boundaries at any time. Many children who are products of hippie homes are able to rise above that environment and become responsible citizens. Others, however, do not grow up, become mature and responsible and leave home. As a matter of fact, they may choose to stay home and bring grandchildren into the home for their parents to raise as little hippies.

- *Hitler Parents*

Hitler homes have very rigid rules. They are so rigid that sixteen-year-olds and eight-year-olds may have the same bedtime. Many of these children leave family stuff behind and are at peace with the world as adults. Others are angry, rebellious, and may have even run away from home as teens.

- *Huxtabel Parents (or Hero Parents)*

Huxtabel (from the Bill Cosby show) homes are structured but flexible. They set rules to meet individual members' needs according to stage and age. Children from Huxtabel homes learn to face the natural consequences of their actions. They are typically successful and happy in adulthood because they have *balance* and *discipline* in their lives. The balance has to do with being healthy in physical, mental, emotional, social, and spiritual ways. The discipline is learning the motto that "you must work before you play." Little Huxtabel children have parents who role model the balance and discipline living.

Roadblock: Abuse

Is your ex a threat to you and/or to your children? If so, *get help*!! Make sure you have told your divorce attorney everything about the abuse. A mental health professional can be invaluable as well. *For the Children's Sake* model is not for situations where abuse is founded.

Roadblock: Parental Alienation Syndrome

If you suspect that your ex is nasty, vindictive, and is using the children to *hurt you*, you need professional help immediately! Keep your attorney apprised about events that make you believe your ex is trying to sabotage your relationship with your child. When you call a mental health professional, ask about her/his competency in working with divorce and parental alienation. It is important for the counselor to meet with *all* family members in *both* homes in order to preserve parent-child relationships and to decrease the psychological harm for your child. During the meantime, do not give up on seeing your child. And, make sure your extended family members are still involved in your child's life.

We Can Parent Together

The pain from old attachment issues has lessened, resolutions have been developed for finances, violence is not threatened, and parental alienation is not occurring. Now, how do you begin this new, business-like relationship? Divorce has forced your family to make structural changes. You are now moving forward with your own healing and ready to get the parenting relationship nailed down.

You must answer an important question to begin with. Are you willing to sit down with your ex-spouse and discuss parenting arrangements?

If you and your former spouse both answered yes, then you are ready to write a **Cooperative Co-parenting Plan.** If your divorce is not final, you can request that this plan be added to the final decree. If it is already final, this plan will still be a great asset to you and your children because it will alleviate many of the parenting difficulties you are having. If you are willing to do this but your former spouse is not, then do it on your own if the divorce is already final. If you have not yet legally divorced, check with your attorney to see if a court order will mandate that you and your ex work together with a qualified mental health professional to hammer out differences and build a parenting plan.

Or, if you or your spouse responded no, then you may be able to develop a **Parallel Co-parenting Plan**. A parallel co-parenting plan is based on the position that the two of you choose to remain disengaged from one another in an effort to keep conflicted interactions at bay. Just beware that when the two of you are not directly communicating with one another your children know it and they may manipulate you in order to obtain more freedom! For example, a teen argues to Mom: "*You know where I was—I was at Dad's.*" Later, the same adolescent says to Dad: "*Sorry I couldn't come see you; I was out of town with Mom.*"

You may have to hire a third party to help you (i.e., mental health professional, mediator, or attorney) write a parallel co-parenting plan. Or, you may be able to use the structure of the cooperative plan delineated below and email your thoughts back and forth until you are able to reach an agreement. Some divorcing or separating parents begin with a parallel co-parental relationship and later are able to move toward a more cooperative spirit. Be open and flexible—this may occur for you.

Developing a Cooperative Co-Parenting Plan

The first thing you have to do is schedule a *staff meeting* for the two of you to meet as parenting business partners. Find a neutral place to meet like a restaurant, coffee shop, library, church office, etc. Decide on a minimum of two hours to conduct this meeting. Stick it out until you complete your plan. The following are the steps that will guide you:

1. Do the following exercise independent of your former spouse. Afterwards, share your responses.

    • The primary concerns I have about parenting are:

    _____

    _____

    _____

    _____

    _____

    _____

    _____

    _____

    _____

- Our child(ren) have said that they need:

_____

_____

_____

_____

_____

_____

_____

_____

- I am willing to make these changes For the Sake of the Children…:

_____

_____

_____

_____

_____

_____

_____

2. Once you both have shared the above statements, reach an agreement on some rules for parenting together between two homes. Write them down! Be precise and be positive. No negative attacks are allowed during this *staff* meeting.

The template below may help the two of you come up with your own statements. All co-parenting plans need to address these:

- Mandate parents as the CEO's; children are children.

- Require that parents live within a reasonable proximity of one another so the child has access to both.

- Be based on the developmental needs of the child (e.g., flexibility, adaptability, attachment, child's sense of time).

- Include a time and means once a week that parents can discuss the children (*staff meeting*).

- Open telephone time with each parent (as long as talk is not self-centered or negative).

- A picture of the other parent in child's room.

- A *mailbox* in each home (to relay to the other parent: child schedules, report card copies, notes, pictures, etc. from child to the other parent). The mailbox is made by each parent separately with the child. Some decorate shoeboxes, etc. to make this mailbox. Parents agree not to use this as their means of communicating negativity to the other parent!

- A calendar displayed where child can see the schedule when he/she will be at the home with mother, father.

- Allow each parent to parent his/her own way.

- Alternate a.m. and p.m. pick-up and drop-off from school and other activities whenever possible to reduce separation anxiety and increase two parent involvements.

- A careful plan will be used to introduce new adult significant others to the children.

- Extended family members will maintain vital roles in the lives of the children.

- When economics allow, children maintain the involvement in extracurricular activities as they did prior to divorce.

- Parents agree on the educational system and medical care of children.

A sample of both a Cooperative Co-Parenting Plan and a Parallel Co-Parenting Plan are included at the end of this section.

3. Once you have written your parenting plan, sign it to make it formal and official!

4. Set up your weekly staff meeting time and place. Make sure you stick to this! Some parents use the telephone rather than meeting face-to-face. Others prefer emails. The important thing is to make sure you have at least a 10-minute interaction each week to address any concerns or necessary weekly changes in the parenting arrangements.

5. Schedule a two-home family meeting with the children. It is preferable for you to meet in a neutral place such as a park, church office, with your family therapist, etc. Tell the children about your new co-parenting plan and how it addresses problems they have expressed. The most important part of this is letting your children know that they have the freedom to be children and that the two of you will remain in the adult roles!

Sample Co-Parenting Plan
(will be signed by both parents)

The Jones Two-Home Family Cooperative Co-parenting Plan

1. I commit to being child-centered.

2. I recognize the importance of living close by my former spouse, for our children's sake.

3. I will not belittle, criticize, or say anything negative about my former spouse in front of our children, by word, body language, or facial expression.

4. I may not agree with my former spouse about all parenting issues, but promise not to judge or condemn him/her as long as abuse is absent.

5. When I see my former spouse in the presence of our children I will speak and act kindly, respectfully, and graciously.

6. If I am dealing with a conflict that may elicit negative emotions with my former spouse, I will speak or meet him/her when the children are nowhere around.

7. I will make every effort to give undivided attention to my children on a consistent basis, listening to them, doing fun things with them, and giving parental support to the best of my ability.

8. I will carefully introduce a new significant other to my children and I will not force my children to immediately bond with this new person.

9. I will tell my children I love them every day, or as often as I see them, and will reassure them that nothing will ever change that. I will use touch and physical affection as other ways to express my love to them.

10. I will not use my children as the go-between with questions or information to or about my former spouse.

11. I will make an attempt to agree with my former spouse on issues of conflict pertaining to the children and will obtain professional help if necessary.

12. I will not say anything negative about my former spouse to friends of family members or any person in the presence of my children.

13. I will seek what is best for my children in all I do, knowing at times that will be very difficult and require self-sacrifice.

14. I will make every effort to cooperate, share, and support my former spouse as the other parent and treat our co-parenting relationship like a *business* one rather than an emotionally-charged or intimate one.

Parent	Parent

Sample Parallel Co-Parenting Plan (will be signed by both parents)

Same as cooperative co-parenting plans with additional statements such as:

1. The conflict with my former spouse is so high that I recognize its potential harm to my children.

Therefore, I agree to a third party as a mediator for pick-ups, drop-offs, and sharing information about our children's schedules and activities.

2. When my former spouse and I contact one another via emails, phone voice mails, etc. I agree to adult privacy and will not allow my children to have access to any of the information.

3. I understand that our children want us both at their extracurricular activities and events. I will stay clear from my former spouse and will do everything I can to keep the atmosphere pleasant for our children.

4. I will not bring our children into the war I have with my former spouse.

5. I will not offer bribes to our children to make me appear as the best or most desirable parent.

Parent	Parent

Congratulations! You Did It!

For the children's sake, you are parenting together after the marriage ended. It may not have been easy but you did it! You have taken off the old marital armor, called a truce, and have written new roles and scripts for your two-home family.

As long as abuse is absent and neither parent has violated their right to be with their children, preserving parent-child relationships is what all children need after their parents divorce. Good luck to you and all members of your family as you grow together.

About the Author

Brenda Dozier, Ph.D., is a Licensed Marriage and Family Therapist, Clinical Member, Former Board Member, and Approved Supervisor of the American Association for Marriage and Family Therapy; a Licensed Professional Counselor and Counseling Supervisor for the Alabama Board of Examiners in Counseling, a part-time instructor at Troy State University in Phenix City, Alabama, a mediator, and a national speaker. She is author of *Two-Home Families: A Family Systems Approach to Divorce Therapy*, a book for mental health profession-als who work with divorced families. Dr. Dozier has also co-authored an article in the *Journal of Divorce and Remarriage* and co-authored an article in *Principles of Parenting* published by the extension service at Auburn University, Auburn, Alabama. She is founder and admin-istrator of Auburn Family Therapy and lives in Auburn, Alabama.

0-595-31726-X